To: ...........................................................................................

From: ...........................................................................

# 365 *Inspirational Thoughts* For Women By Women

THE HOLY BIBLE, NEW INTERNATIONAL VERSION®, NIV® Copyright © 1973, 1978, 1984, 2011 by Biblica, Inc.™ Used by permission of Biblica, Inc.™ All rights reserved worldwide. Biblica, transforming lives through God's Word. The Message © 1993, 1994, 1995, 1996. Used by permission of NavPress Publishing Group. The Living Bible (TLB) © 1971. Used by permission of Tyndale House Publishers, Inc., Wheaton, Illinois 60189. All rights reserved.

Except for Scripture verses, references to men and masculine pronouns have been replaced with "people," "women," and gender-neutral or feminine pronouns.

Every attempt has been made to locate accurate names, descriptions and birth dates for those women quoted in this book.

Photo © kukuruxa/Shutterstock
Image/WitchEra/2011 Used under license from Shutterstock.com

All rights reserved. No part of this publication may be reproduced, stored in a retrieval system or transmitted in any form by any means—electronic, mechanical, photocopying, recording, or any other—without the prior written permission of the publisher.

Made in China

# January 1

Only a night from old to new,
Only a sleep from night to morn.
The new is but the old come true,
Each sunrise sees a new year born.

HELEN HUNT JACKSON
1830-1855, AMERICAN WRITER

*He put a new song in my mouth, A hymn of praise to our God.*
*Many will see and fear And put their trust in the Lord.*

PSALM 40:3 NIV

# December 31

I said to a man who stood at the gate of the year,
"Give me a light that I may tread safely into the unknown." And he replied, "Go out into the darkness and put your hand in the hand of God. That shall be to you better than a light and safer than a known way."

M. Louise Haskins
1875–1957, British writer, lecturer;
reply by King George VI

# January 2

How much of our lives are…well…so daily. How often our hours are filled with the mundane, seemingly unimportant things that have to be done, whether at home or work. These very "daily" tasks could become a celebration of praise. "It is through consecration," someone has said, "that drudgery is made divine."

GIGI GRAHAM TCHIVIDJIAN
1945–, AMERICAN WRITER, SPEAKER, D. BILLY GRAHAM

# December 30

Live for today but hold your hands open to tomorrow. Anticipate the future and its changes with joy. There is a seed of God's love in every event, every circumstance, every unpleasant situation in which you may find yourself.

Barbara Johnson
1927-2007 American Writer, Speaker

# January 3

A joyful heart is like a sunshine of God's love,
the hope of eternal happiness, a burning flame
of God....And if we pray, we will become that
sunshine of God's love—in our own home,
the place where we live, and in the world at large.

MOTHER TERESA OF CALCUTTA
1910-1997, ROMAN CATHOLIC NUN,
NOBEL PEACE PRIZE WINNER

# December 29

If I can stop one heart from breaking,
I shall not live in vain:
If I can ease one life the aching,
Or cool one pain,
Or help one fainting robin
Unto his nest again,
I shall not live in vain.

EMILY DICKINSON
1830-1886, AMERICAN POET

# January 4

None of us knows what the next change is going to be, what unexpected opportunity is just around the corner, waiting to change all the tenor of our lives.

KATHLEEN NORRIS
1947-, AMERICAN WRITER

# December 28

Wholehearted, ready laughter heals, encourages, relaxes anyone within hearing distance. The laughter that springs from love makes wide the space around it—gives room for the loved one to enter in. Real laughter welcomes, and never shuts out.

Eugenia Price
1916-1996, American writer

# January 5

I avoid looking forward or backward, and try to keep looking upward.

Charlotte Brontë
1816-1855, British writer

*If I rise on the wings of the dawn, if I settle on the far side of the sea, even there Your hand will guide me, Your right hand will hold me fast.*

PSALM 139:9-10 NIV

# December 27

God's gifts put man's best dreams to shame.

ELIZABETH BARRETT BROWNING
1806–1861, BRITISH POET

*Let us not get tired of doing what is right,
for after a while we will reap a harvest of blessing.*

GALATIANS 6:9 TLB

# January 6

God bless you and utterly satisfy your heart...with Himself.

Amy Carmichael
1867-1951, Irish missionary to India, poet

# December 26

When we put people before possessions in our hearts,
we are sowing seeds of enduring satisfaction.

Beverly LaHaye
1929–, American writer

# January 7

I know that God is faithful.
I know that He answers prayers,
many times in ways I may not understand.

Sheila Walsh
1956–, American singer, speaker

# December 25

The coming of Jesus at Bethlehem brought joy to the world and to every human heart. May His coming this Christmas bring to each one of us that peace and joy that He desires to give.

Mother Teresa of Calcutta
1910-1997, Roman Catholic nun,
Nobel Peace Prize winner

# January 8

I do not ask for any crown
But that which all may win;
Nor try to conquer any world
Except the one within.

Louisa May Alcott
1832-1888, American writer

# December 24

Angels and archangels may have gathered there,
Cherubim and seraphim thronged the air;
But His mother only, in her maiden bliss,
Worshipped the Beloved with a kiss.

CHRISTINA ROSSETTI
1830-1894, BRITISH POET, LYRICIST

# January 9

All my life through, the new sights of nature made me rejoice like a child.

MARIE CURIE
1867-1934, POLISH-BORN FRENCH PHYSICIST

# December 23

God must have said, "I know what I'll do,
I'll send my LOVE right down there where they are.
And I'll send it as a tiny baby, so they'll have to
touch it, and they'll have to hold it close."

GLORIA GAITHER
1942–, AMERICAN WRITER, SINGER/SONGWRITER

# January 10

Live your life while you have it.
Life is a splendid gift—
there is nothing small about it.

Florence Nightingale
1820-1910, British nurse, hospital reformer

*Give away your life; you'll find life given back, but not merely given back—given back with bonus and blessing. Giving, not getting, is the way. Generosity begets generosity.*

LUKE 6:38 The Message

# December 22

God grant you the light in Christmas,
which is faith; the warmth of Christmas,
which is love...the all of Christmas, which is Christ.

WILDA ENGLISH
AMERICAN WRITER

*We all live off His generous bounty, gift after gift after gift.... This exuberant giving and receiving, this endless knowing and understanding—all this came through Jesus, the Messiah.*

JOHN 1:16-17 THE MESSAGE

# January 11

Face your deficiencies and acknowledge them; but do not let them master you. Let them teach you patience, sweetness, insight. When we do the best we can, we never know what miracle is wrought in our life, or in the life of another.

HELEN KELLER
1880-1968, AMERICAN WRITER,
CRUSADER FOR THE HANDICAPPED

# December 21

We expect too much at Christmas.
It's got to be magical. It's got to go right.
Feasting. Fun. The perfect present.
All that anticipation. Take it easy.
Love's the thing. The rest is tinsel.

PAM BROWN
1948–, AUSTRALIAN WRITER

# January 12

Everything which relates to God is infinite.
We must therefore, while we keep our hearts humble,
keep our aims high. Our highest services are indeed
but finite, imperfect. But as God is unlimited in
goodness, He should have our unlimited love.

Hannah More
1745-1833, British writer, social reformer

# December 20

Christmas, my child, is love in action.... When you love someone, you give to them, as God gives to us. The greatest gift He ever gave was the person of His Son, sent to us in human form so that we might know what God the Father is really like! Every time we love, every time we give, it's Christmas.

DALE EVANS ROGERS
1912-2001, AMERICAN ACTOR, M. ROY ROGERS

# January 13

Look at a day when you are supremely satisfied at the end....It's when you've had everything to do and you've done it.

MARGARET THATCHER
1925-, FORMER PRIME MINISTER OF GREAT BRITAIN

# December 19

This is the real gift: we have been given the breath of life, designed with a unique, one-of-a-kind soul that exists forever—whether we live it as burden or a joy or with indifference doesn't change the fact that we've been given the gift of being now and forever. Priceless in value, we are handcrafted by God, who has a personal design and plan for each one of us.

WENDY MOORE
1971–, AMERICAN WRITER

# January 14

There is nothing I would not do
for those who are really my friends.
I have no notion of loving people by halves.

JANE AUSTEN
1775-1817, BRITISH WRITER

# December 18

The future belongs to those who believe
in the beauty of their dreams.

ELEANOR ROOSEVELT
1884–1962, AMERICAN FIRST LADY, HUMANITARIAN

*No eye has seen, nor ear heard, nor the human heart conceived,*
*what God has prepared for those who love Him.*

I CORINTHIANS 2:9 NRSV

# January 15

**I am not afraid...**
**I was born to do this.**

JOAN OF ARC
1412-1431, FRENCH PATRIOT AND MARTYR

*No test or temptation that comes your way is beyond the course of what others have had to face. All you need to remember is that God will never let you down; He'll never let you be pushed past your limit; He'll always be there to help you come through it.*

I CORINTHIANS 10:13 THE MESSAGE

# December 17

Certain springs are tapped only when we are alone....Women need solitude in order to find again the true essence of themselves; that firm strand which will be the indispensable center of a whole web of human relationships.

Anne Morrow Lindbergh
1906-2001, American writer; m. Charles Lindbergh

# January 16

Courage is the price that life exacts for granting peace. The soul that knows it not, knows no release from little things.

AMELIA EARHART
1897–1937, AMERICAN AVIATOR, WRITER

# December 16

Prayer is such an ordinary, everyday, mundane thing. Certainly, people who pray are no more saints than the rest of us. Rather, they are people who want to share a life with God, to love and be loved, to speak and to listen, to work and to be at rest in the presence of God.

Roberta Bondi
Contemporary, American educator, writer

# January 17

The soul is a breath of living spirit, that with excellent sensitivity, permeates the entire body to give it life. Just so, the breath of the air makes the earth fruitful. Thus the air is the soul of the earth, moistening it, greening it.

Hildegard of Bingen
1098–1179, German nun, Christian poet

# December 15

God, with all His giving heart,
can only give us Himself as we recognize
the depth of the need in our own lives.

Eugenia Price
1916–1996, American writer

# January 18

"Hope" is the thing with feathers—
That perches in the soul—
And sings the tune without the words—
And never stops—at all.

EMILY DICKINSON
1830-1886, AMERICAN POET

# December 14

Character cannot be developed in ease and quiet. Only through experience of trial and suffering can the soul be strengthened, vision cleared, ambition inspired, and success achieved.

Helen Keller
1880–1968, American writer,
crusader for the handicapped

# January 19

Each one of us is God's special work of art. Through us, He teaches and inspires, delights and encourages, informs and uplifts all those who view our lives. God, the master artist, is most concerned about expressing Himself—His thoughts and His intentions—through what He paints in our character.... [He] wants to paint a beautiful portrait of His Son in and through your life. A painting like no other in all of time.

Joni Eareckson Tada
1949-, American writer, speaker

# December 13

If facts are the seeds that later produce knowledge and wisdom, then the emotions and the impressions of the senses are the fertile soil in which the seeds must grow.

RACHEL CARSON
1907-1964, AMERICAN BIOLOGIST, WRITER

*Listen...be wise, and keep your heart on the right path.*

PROVERBS 23:19 NIV

# January 20

It doesn't take monumental feats to make the world a better place. It can be as simple as letting someone go ahead of you in a grocery line.

BARBARA JOHNSON
1927-2007, AMERICAN WRITER, SPEAKER

*You're blessed when you care. At the moment of being "care-full," you find yourselves cared for. You're blessed when you get your inside world—your mind and heart—put right. Then you can see God in the outside world.*

MATTHEW 5:7-8 THE MESSAGE

# December 12

Cherish your human connections:
your relationships with friends and family.

Barbara Bush
1925-, American First Lady

# January 21

As parents, we must be convinced
of our beliefs. We must know where
we stand, so that our children
will know where they stand.

Kim Boyce
1963–, American singer, writer

# December 11

**If God sends us on stony paths, He provides strong shoes.**

CORRIE TEN BOOM
1892–1983, DUTCH EVANGELIST, WRITER

# January 22

If you believe in a God who controls
the big things, you have to believe in a God
who controls the little things. It is we, of course,
to whom things look "little" or "big."

ELISABETH ELLIOT
1926–, AMERICAN WRITER,
M. MARTYRED MISSIONARY JIM ELLIOT

# December 10

Reach out and care for someone who needs the touch of hospitality. The time you spend caring today will be a love gift that will blossom into the fresh joy of God's Spirit in the future.

Emilie Barnes
1938–, American speaker, writer

# January 23

Some people give time, some money, some their skills and connections; some literally give their blood...but everyone has something to give.

Barbara Bush
1925–, American First Lady

# December 9

Yes, I have doubted. I have wandered off the path. I have been lost. But I always returned. It is beyond the logic I seek. It is intuitive—an intrinsic, built-in sense of direction. I seem always to find my way home. My faith has wavered but has saved me.

Helen Hayes
1900–1993, American actor

# January 24

Whatever my individual desires were to be free, I was not alone. There were many others who felt the same way.

ROSA PARKS
1913–2005, AMERICAN CIVIL RIGHTS ACTIVIST

# December 8

So where do you go when you can't fix your life?
The only place to go is back to the One who made you.

SHEILA WALSH
1956–, AMERICAN SINGER, SPEAKER

*Pray to the Father. He loves to help. You'll get His help, and won't be condescended to when you ask for it. Ask boldly, believing, without a second thought.*

JAMES 1:5–6 THE MESSAGE

# January 25

God is bigger than any disability.
Love Him, appreciate His blessings,
and trust Him for the rest of the journey.
He puts the rainbow at the end of the hardest trail.

Dale Evans Rogers
1912-2001, American actor, m. Roy Rogers

# December 7

Genius is the gold in the mine;
talent is the miner that
works and brings it out.

Lady Marguerite Blessington
1789–1849, British writer

# January 26

There must always be a remedy for wrong and injustice if we only know how to find it.

Ida B. Wells
1862-1931, African-American journalist and activist

*Without God, it is utterly impossible. But with God everything is possible.*

MARK 10:27 TLB

# December 6

I see God as all-perfect, all-complete, all-powerful. God is love. I believe man is created in God's image. It makes a difference in a novel whether the writer believes we are created in God's image or whether we create God in our own.

FLANNERY O'CONNOR
1925-1964, AMERICAN WRITER

# January 27

What a strange thing is memory, and hope;
one looks backward, the other forward. The one
is of today, the other is of tomorrow. Memory is
history recorded in our brain, memory is a painter,
it paints pictures of the past and of the day.

Grandma Moses (Anna Mary Robertson)
1860-1961, American artist

# December 5

Tuck [this] thought into your heart today. Treasure it. Your Father God cares about your daily everythings that concern you.

Kay Arthur
1933-, American writer

# January 28

We cannot always understand the ways of Almighty God—the crosses which He sends us, the sacrifices which He demands of us.... But we accept with faith and resignation His holy will with no looking back to what might have been, and we are at peace.

Rose Fitzgerald Kennedy
1890-1995, mother of John F. Kennedy

# December 4

One of the most wonderful things about knowing God is that there's always so much more to know, so much more to discover. Just when we least expect it, He intrudes into our neat and tidy notions about who He is and how He works.

JONI EARECKSON TADA
1949–, AMERICAN WRITER, SPEAKER

# January 29

We live in the present,
we dream of the future,
but we learn eternal truths
from the past.

Lucy Maud Montgomery
1874-1942, Canadian writer

# December 3

Truth is always exciting.
Speak it, then. Life is dull without it.

PEARL S. BUCK
1892-1973, AMERICAN WRITER, NOBEL PRIZE WINNER

*What you say goes, God, and stays, as permanent as the heavens. Your truth never goes out of fashion; it's up-to-date as the earth when the sun comes up. Your Word and truth are dependable as ever.*

PSALM 119:89-91 THE MESSAGE

# January 30

Action is indeed the sole medium of expression for ethics.

JANE ADDAMS
1860-1935, AMERICAN SOCIAL REFORMER,
NOBEL PRIZE WINNER

*Therefore, as we have opportunity, let us do good to all people.*

GALATIANS 6:10 NIV

# December 2

For attractive lips, speak words of kindness. For lovely eyes, seek out the good in people. For a slim figure, share your food with the hungry. For beautiful hair, let a child run his or her fingers through it once a day. For poise, walk with the knowledge you'll never walk alone.

Audrey Hepburn
1929-1993, Belgian actor

# January 31

[Astronomical] observations...
are peculiarly adapted to women....
The eye that directs a needle in the delicate
meshes of embroidery will equally well bisect a
star with the spider web of the micrometer.

MARIA MITCHELL
1818–1889, AMERICAN ASTRONOMER, EDUCATOR

# December 1

Prayer is the deliberate and persevering action of the soul. It is true and enduring, and full of grace. Prayer fastens the soul to God and makes it one with God's will.

JULIAN OF NORWICH
1342-1413, BRITISH CHRISTIAN

# February 1

I don't know that there are
any short cuts to doing a good job.

Sandra Day O'Connor
1930–, American Supreme Court Justice

# November 30

To be rooted is perhaps the most important and least recognized need of the human soul.

SIMONE WEIL
1909-1943, FRENCH REVOLUTIONARY, PHILOSOPHER

# February 2

**Light tomorrow with today!**

Elizabeth Barrett Browning
1806–1861, British poet

*Faith is being sure of what we hope for and certain of what we do not see.*

HEBREWS 11:1 NIV

# November 29

Tradition gives us a sense of solidarity and roots,
a knowing there are some things one can count on.

Gloria Gaither
1942–, American writer, singer/songwriter

# February 3

Peace is not placidity: peace is the power to endure the megatron of pain with joy, the silent thunder of release, the ordering of love. Peace is the atom's start, the primal image: God within the heart.

MADELEINE L'ENGLE
1918-2007, AMERICAN WRITER

# November 28

I pray hard, work hard and leave the rest to God.

Florence Griffith Joyner
1959–, American track athlete

# February 4

Practice means to perform,
over and over again in the face of all obstacles,
some act of vision, of faith, of desire. Practice is
a means of inviting the perfection desired.

MARTHA GRAHAM
1894–1991, AMERICAN DANCER, CHOREOGRAPHER, EDUCATOR

# November 27

Gratitude is the memory of the heart;
therefore forget not to say often,
I have all I ever enjoyed.

Lydia Marie Child
1802-1880, American abolitionist, writer

*Oh, give thanks to the Lord, for He is good;*
*His love and His kindness go on forever.*

I CHRONICLES 16:34 TLB

# February 5

When you get into a tight place and everything goes against you, till it seems as though you could not hang on a minute longer, never give up then, for that is just the place and time that the tide will turn.

Harriet Beecher Stowe
1811-1896, American writer

# November 26

I learned three important things in college—
to use a library, to memorize quickly and visually,
to drop asleep at any time given a horizontal
surface and fifteen minutes. What I could not
learn was to think creatively on schedule.

Agnes DeMille
1905–1993, American dancer, choreographer

# February 6

The greatness of the human personality begins at the hour of birth. From this...affirmation there comes what may seem a strange conclusion: that education must start from birth.

Maria Montessori
1870-1952, Italian educator, physician,
originator Montessori Method

# November 25

Faith is the first factor in a life devoted to service.
Without faith, nothing is possible.
With it, nothing is impossible.

Mary McLeod Bethune
1875-1955, American educator, writer

# February 7

Believe in yourself, learn, and never stop wanting to build a better world.

MARY MCLEOD BETHUNE
1875–1955, AMERICAN EDUCATOR, WRITER

*Encourage each other to build each other up, just as you are already doing.*

I THESSALONIANS 5:11 TLB

# November 24

Please know that I am aware of the hazards.
I want to do it because I want to do it. Women must
try to do things as men have tried. When they fail,
their failure must be a challenge to others.

Amelia Earhart
1897-1937, American aviator, writer

# February 8

This is my letter to the world,
That never wrote to me,
The simple news that Nature told,
With tender majesty.
Her message is committed,
To hands I cannot see;
For love of her, sweet countrymen,
Judge tenderly of me.

Emily Dickinson
1830-1886, American poet

# November 23

Taking joy in life is a woman's best cosmetic.

Rosalind Russell
1907-1976, American actor

*Instead of looking at the fashions, walk out into the fields and look at the wildflowers. They never primp or shop, but have you ever seen color and design quite like it?... If God gives such attention to the appearance of wildflowers...don't you think He'll attend to you?*

Matthew 6:28-30 The Message

# February 9

The wonder of our Lord is that He is so accessible to us in the common things of our lives: the cup of water...breaking of the bread... welcoming children into our arms...fellowship over a meal...giving thanks. A simple attitude of caring, listening, and lovingly telling the truth.

NANCIE CARMICHAEL
CONTEMPORARY, AMERICAN WRITER, SINGER/SONGWRITER

# November 22

It does not so much matter what happens.
It is what one does when it happens that really counts.

Laura Ingalls Wilder
1867-1957, American children's writer

# February 10

God, with all His giving heart,
can only give us Himself as we recognize
the depth of the need in our own lives.

EUGENIA PRICE
1916-1996, AMERICAN WRITER

# November 21

God's designs regarding you,
and His methods of bringing about
these designs, are infinitely wise.

MADAME JEANNE GUYON
1648–1717, FRENCH CHRISTIAN

# February 11

You gain strength, courage
and confidence by every experience in which
you really stop to look fear in the face.
You must do the thing you think you cannot do.

Eleanor Roosevelt
1884-1962, American First Lady, humanitarian

# November 20

Parents can only give good advice or put them on the right paths, but the final forming of a person's character lies in their own hands.

ANNE FRANK
1929-1945, GERMAN JEWISH DIARIST

# February 12

Never doubt that a small group of thoughtful, committed citizens can change the world. Indeed, it is the only thing that ever has.

MARGARET MEAD
1901-1978, AMERICAN ANTHROPOLOGIST, WRITER

*Nothing is impossible with God.*

LUKE 1:37 NIV

# November 19

For what I have received may the Lord make me truly thankful. And more truly for what I have not received.

STORM (MARGARET) JAMESON
1891–1986, BRITISH WRITER

*God can pour on the blessings in astonishing ways so that you're ready for anything and everything.*

II CORINTHIANS 9:8 THE MESSAGE

# February 13

I am for lifting everyone off the social bottom. In fact, I am for doing away with the social bottom altogether.

Clare Boothe Luce
1903-1987, American diplomat, politician

# November 18

If you surrender completely to the moments as they pass, you live more richly those moments.

ANNE MORROW LINDBERGH
1906-2001, AMERICAN WRITER; M. CHARLES LINDBERGH

# February 14

We learn to believe by believing. We learn to love by loving. The practice of acting on a certain thing, even (or especially) when feeling is absent, embodies the entire "how" of growth.

EUGENIA PRICE
1916–1996, AMERICAN WRITER

# November 17

I thank God that… [He] has raised up for Himself a people who are acting, in no small degree, up to the light which they have received.

Catherine Booth
1829-1890, British evangelist,
first woman Salvation Army general

# February 15

It is the simple things of life that make living worthwhile, the sweet fundamental things such as love and duty, work and rest, and living close to nature.

LAURA INGALLS WILDER
1867–1957, AMERICAN CHILDREN'S WRITER

*Every good and perfect gift is from above, coming down from the Father of the heavenly lights, who does not change like shifting shadows.*

JAMES 1:17 NIV

# November 16

Oh, the comfort—the inexpressible comfort of feeling safe with a person—having neither to weigh thoughts nor measure words, but pouring them all right out, just as they are, chaff and grain together; certain that a faithful hand will take and sift them, keep what is worth keeping, and then with the breath of kindness blow the rest away.

DINAH MARIA MULOCK CRAIK
1826-1887, ENGLISH WRITER

# February 16

If all were rain and never sun,
No bow could span the hill;
If all were sun and never rain,
There'd be no rainbow still.

Christina Rossetti
1830–1894, British poet, lyricist

# November 15

For women there are, undoubtedly, great difficulties in the path, but so much the more to overcome. First, no woman should say, "I am but a woman!" But a woman! What more can you ask to be?

MARIA MITCHELL
1818-1889, AMERICAN ASTRONOMER, EDUCATOR

# February 17

The center of power is not to be found
in summit meetings or in peace conferences.
It is not in Peking or Washington or the United
Nations, but rather where a child of God prays
in the power of the Spirit for God's will to be done
in her life, in her home, and in the world about her.

Ruth Bell Graham
1920-2007, American writer, m. Billy Graham

# November 14

We can do no great things,
only small things with great love.

MOTHER TERESA OF CALCUTTA
1910–1997, ROMAN CATHOLIC NUN,
NOBEL PEACE PRIZE WINNER

# February 18

If only the next step is clear,
then the one thing to do is take it!
Don't pledge your Lord or yourself
to any steps beyond what you know.
You don't see them yet.

AMY CARMICHAEL
1867-1951, IRISH MISSIONARY TO INDIA, POET

# November 13

What is success? I think it is a mixture of having a flair for the thing that you are doing; knowing that it is not enough, that you have got to have hard work and a certain sense of purpose.

MARGARET THATCHER
1925–, FORMER PRIME MINISTER OF GREAT BRITAIN

# February 19

It is never enough to know about spiritual things with your mind. Mental knowledge is not the same thing as truly understanding from the center of your being, which results from experiencing and doing.

Teresa of Avila
1515–1582, Spanish Christian writer

# November 12

Life is either a daring adventure
or nothing at all. Security is mostly
a superstition. It does not exist in nature.

HELEN KELLER
1880-1968, AMERICAN WRITER,
CRUSADER FOR THE HANDICAPPED

# February 20

When one door of happiness closes, another opens; but often we look so long at the closed door that we do not see the one which has been opened for us.

HELEN KELLER
1880–1968, AMERICAN WRITER,
CRUSADER FOR THE HANDICAPPED

*"For I know the plans I have for you," declares the Lord, "plans to prosper you and not to harm you, plans to give you hope and a future."*

JEREMIAH 29:11 NIV

# November 11

So wait before the Lord. Wait in the stillness. And in that stillness, assurance will come to you. You will know that you are heard; you will know that your Lord ponders the voice of your humble desires; you will hear quiet words spoken to you yourself, perhaps to your grateful surprise and refreshment.

Amy Carmichael
1867–1951, Irish missionary to India, poet

# February 21

The measure of a life, after all,
is not its duration but its donation.

Corrie ten Boom
1892–1983, Dutch evangelist, writer

# November 10

A child her wayward pencil drew
On margins of her book;
Garlands of flower, dancing elves,
Bud, butterfly, and brook,
Lessons undone, and plum forgot,
Seeking with hand and heart
The teacher whom she learned to love
Before she knew t'was Art.

LOUISA MAY ALCOTT
1832-1888, AMERICAN WRITER

# February 22

No one can arrive from being talented alone.
God gives talent, work transforms talent into genius.

Anna Pavlova
1881-1931, Russian ballerina

# November 9

Miracles are instantaneous,
they cannot be summoned,
but come of themselves,
usually at unlikely moments and to
those who least expect them.

Katherine Anne Porter
1890-1980, American writer

*He performs wonders that cannot be fathomed,*
*miracles that cannot be counted.*

JOB 5:9 NIV

# February 23

Eternity is not something
that begins after you are dead.
It is going on all the time.
We are in it now.

Charlotte Perkins Gilman
1860–1935, American writer, social critic

# November 8

Ideal conversation must be an exchange of thought, and not, as many of those who worry most about their shortcomings believe, an eloquent exhibition of wit or oratory.

EMILY POST
1873-1960, AMERICAN WRITER, SOCIALITE

# February 24

To love God, to serve Him because we love Him, is... our highest happiness. Love makes all labor light. We serve with enthusiasm where we love with sincerity.

Hannah More
1745-1833, British writer, social reformer

# November 7

If it is God who gives prayer, then God often gives it in the form of gratitude, and gratitude itself, when it is received attentively in prayer, is healing to the heart. Prayer is such a mysterious business for something so ordinary and everyday.

Roberta Bondi
Contemporary, American educator, writer

# February 25

Blues are the songs of despair,
but gospel songs are the songs of hope.

MAHALIA JACKSON
1911–1972, AMERICAN GOSPEL SINGER

*May the God of hope fill you with all joy and peace in believing, so that you may abound in hope.*

ROMANS 15:13 NIV

# November 6

There is this important difference between
love and friendship: while the former delights in
extremes and opposites, the latter demands equalities.

Madame de Maintenon
1635-1719, French queen

# February 26

Always stay connected to people
and seek out things that bring you joy.
Dream with abandon. Pray confidently.

Barbara Johnson
1927–2007, American Writer, Speaker

# November 5

Encouragement is being a good listener,
being positive, letting others know you accept
them for who they are. It is offering hope,
caring about the feelings of another, understanding.

GIGI GRAHAM TCHIVIDJIAN
1945–, AMERICAN WRITER, SPEAKER, D. BILLY GRAHAM

# February 27

There isn't a man or a woman anywhere, I am convinced, who does not long for tenderness.

ELISABETH ELLIOT
1926–, AMERICAN WRITER,
M. MARTYRED MISSIONARY JIM ELLIOT

# November 4

Opinion is a flitting thing,
But Truth outlasts the Sun—
If then we cannot own them both—
Possess the oldest one.

EMILY DICKINSON
1830-1886, AMERICAN POET

*I have chosen the way of truth; I have set my heart on Your laws....*
*I run in the path of Your commands, for You have set my heart free.*

PSALM 119:30, 32 NIV

# February 28

Before anything else, above all else,
beyond everything else, God loves us.
God loves us extravagantly, ridiculously,
without limit or condition. God is in
love with us...God yearns for us.

Roberta Bondi
Contemporary, American educator, writer

# November 3

Let us love so well our work
shall still be better for our love,
and still our love be better for our work.

ELIZABETH BARRETT BROWNING
1806-1861, BRITISH POET

# February 29

Women, if the soul of the nation is to be saved,
I believe that you must become its soul.

Coretta Scott King
1927–2006, American civil rights activist, writer

# November 2

God is every moment totally aware of each one of us. Totally aware in intense concentration and love.... No one passes through any area of life, happy or tragic, without the attention of God with him.

Eugenia Price
1916–1996, American writer

# March 1

**Do what you can to show you care about other people, and you will make our world a better place.**

ROSALYNN CARTER
1927–, AMERICAN FIRST LADY

*Love others as you love yourself. That's an act of true freedom.*

GALATIANS 5:14 THE MESSAGE

# November 1

Faith has to be exercised in the midst of ordinary, down-to-earth living.

ELISABETH ELLIOT
M. MARTYRED MISSIONARY JIM ELLIOT

# March 2

For me it's the challenge—the challenge to try to beat myself or do better than I did in the past. I try to keep in mind not what I have accomplished but what I have to try to accomplish in the future.

Jackie Joyner Kersee
1962-, American Olympic gold medalist

# October 31

We are each other's harvest;
we are each other's business;
we are each other's magnitude and bond.

GWENDOLYN BROOKS
1917-2000, AMERICAN POET, WRITER

# March 3

The story of a love is not important—what is important is that one is capable of love. It is perhaps the only glimpse we are permitted of eternity.

Helen Hayes
1900–1993, American actor

# October 30

It is an extraordinary and beautiful thing that God, in creation...works with the beauty of matter; the reality of things; the discoveries of the senses, all five of them; so that we, in turn, may hear the grass growing; see a face springing to life in love and laughter.... The offerings of creation...our glimpses of truth.

Madeleine L'Engle
1918-2007, American writer

# March 4

I have suffered a lot from both
physical and emotional pain.
Sometimes I thought I could not live,
but God saved me and gave me faith and hope.

Kim Phuc
1963–, Vietnam War survivor of Napalm bomb

# October 29

How wonderful it is that nobody need wait a single moment before starting to improve the world.

Anne Frank
1929–1945, German Jewish diarist

# March 5

We may run, walk, stumble, drive, or fly,
but let us never lose sight of the reason for the journey,
or miss a chance to see a rainbow on the way.

Gloria Gaither
1942–, American writer, singer/songwriter

# October 28

Whether we are poets or parents or teachers or artists or gardeners, we must start where we are and use what we have. In the process of creation and relationship, what seems mundane and trivial may show itself to be holy, precious, part of a pattern.

LUCI SHAW
1928–, AMERICAN WRITER

# March 6

In every outthrust headland, in every curving beach, in every grain of sand there is a story of the earth.

RACHEL CARSON
1907–1964, AMERICAN BIOLOGIST, WRITER

*What a wildly wonderful world, God! You made it all, with Wisdom at Your side, made earth overflow with your wonderful creations.*

PSALM 104:24 THE MESSAGE

# October 27

Some people regard discipline as a chore.
For me, it is a kind of order that sets me free to fly.

JULIE ANDREWS
1935–, BRITISH SINGER, ACTOR

*So, chosen by God for this new life of love,*
*dress in the wardrobe God picked out for you:*
*compassion, kindness, humility, quiet strength, discipline.*

COLOSSIANS 3:12 THE MESSAGE

# March 7

Who can measure the advantages that would result if the magnificent abilities of women… could be devoted to the needs of government, society, home, instead of being consumed in the struggle to obtain their birthright of individual freedom?

SUSAN B. ANTHONY
1820-1906, AMERICAN SUFFRAGIST

# October 26

Spread love everywhere you go: first of all in your own home. Give love to your children, to a wife or husband, to a next-door neighbor.

MOTHER TERESA OF CALCUTTA
NOBEL PEACE PRIZE WINNER

# March 8

Just opening up the door, having this ordinary person fly, says a lot for the future. You can always equate astronauts with explorers who were subsidized. Now you are getting someone going just to observe. And then you'll have the settlers.

CHRISTA MCAULIFFE
1948-1986, AMERICAN EDUCATOR,
MEMBER OF SPACE SHUTTLE CHALLENGER

# October 25

As a mother, my job is to take care of what is possible and trust God with the impossible.

Ruth Bell Graham
1920–2007, American writer, m. Billy Graham

# March 9

Heavenly Father, speak to me today concerning how to reach out to the world. From the youngest to the oldest, there is something we all can do.

Kim Boyce
1963–, American singer, writer

# October 24

Real education should educate us out of self into something far finer—into a selflessness which links us with all humanity.

Lady Nancy Astor
1879-1964, British, first woman Member of Parliament

# March 10

We hold these truths to be self-evident:
that all men and women are created equal.

ELIZABETH CADY STANTON
1815–1902, AMERICAN SUFFRAGIST, SOCIAL REFORMER

# October 23

In order to realize the worth of the anchor,
we need to feel the stress of the storm.

CORRIE TEN BOOM
1892-1983, DUTCH EVANGELIST, WRITER

# March 11

No matter what the circumstances are,
it is best to pursue behavior that is above reproach,
because then you will be respected for your actions.

ROSA PARKS
1913-2005, AMERICAN CIVIL RIGHTS ACTIVIST

*Be content with who you are, and don't put on airs.*
*God's strong hand is on you; He'll promote you at the right time.*
*Live carefree before God; He is most careful with you.*

I PETER 5:6-7 THE MESSAGE

# October 22

The well of Providence is deep.
It's the buckets we bring to it that are small.

Mary Webb
1881–1927, Scottish religious leader, writer, poet

*May your roots go down deep into the soil of God's marvelous love; and may you be able to feel and understand…how long, how wide, how deep and how high His love really is.*

Ephesians 3:17–18 TLB

# March 12

You cannot hope to build a better world without improving the individuals. To that end each of us must work for her own improvement, and at the same time share a general responsibility for all humanity, our particular duty being to aid those to whom we think we can be most useful.

Marie Curie
1867-1934, Polish-born French physicist

# October 21

We have all known the long loneliness and
we have learned that the only solution is love
and that love comes with community.

DOROTHY DAY
1897-1980, AMERICAN WRITER, SOCIAL REFORMER

# March 13

Our feelings do not affect God's facts. They may blow up, like clouds, and cover the eternal things that we do most truly believe. We may not see the shining of the promises—but they still shine! [His strength] is not for one moment less because of our human weakness.

AMY CARMICHAEL
1867-1951, IRISH MISSIONARY TO INDIA, POET

# October 20

You have to look for the joy. Look for the light of God that is hitting your life, and you will find sparkles you didn't know were there.

BARBARA JOHNSON
1927-2007, AMERICAN WRITER, SPEAKER

# March 14

Prayer unites the soul to God, for although the soul may always be like God in nature and substance, it is often unlike Him in condition.

Julian of Norwich
1342-1413, British Christian

# October 19

Life begets life. Energy creates energy.
It is by spending oneself that one becomes rich.

Sarah Bernhardt
1844–1923, French actor

# March 15

I am not writing just for the sake of writing. I have attempted to convey...a message, which God has given, and to convey that message with whatever abilities were given to me. Whatever I've been able to accomplish has been God's doing. I've tried to follow His teachings in all my writing and thoughts.

Grace Livingston Hill
1865-1947, American writer

# October 18

There is nothing so kingly as kindness,
And nothing so royal as truth.

ALICE CARY
1820–1871, AMERICAN POET

# March 16

Good communication is as stimulating
as black coffee, and just as hard to sleep after.

Anne Morrow Lindbergh
1906–2001, American writer; m. Charles Lindbergh

# October 17

The true way of softening one's troubles
is to solace those of others.

MADAME DE MAINTENON
1635–1719, FRENCH QUEEN

*Our hearts ache, but at the same time we have the joy of the Lord. We are poor, but we give rich spiritual gifts to others. We own nothing, and yet we enjoy everything.*

II CORINTHIANS 6:10 TLB

# March 17

In spite of everything I still believe that people are really good at heart. I simply can't build up my hopes on a foundation consisting of confusion, misery and death.

Anne Frank
1929-1945, German Jewish diarist

# October 16

People see God every day.
They just don't recognize Him.

Pearl Bailey
1918–1990, American singer

# March 18

The secret of joy in work
is contained in one word—excellence.
To know how to do something well is to enjoy it.

Pearl S. Buck
1892-1973, American writer, Nobel Prize winner

*In everything you do, put God first,*
*and He will direct you and crown your efforts with success.*

PROVERBS 3:6 TLB

# October 15

A woman is like a teabag; you can't tell how strong she is until you put her in hot water.

Nancy Reagan
1921–, American First Lady, actor

# March 19

I have learned from experience that the greater part of our happiness or misery depends on our dispositions and not on our circumstances.

Martha Washington
1732-1802, American First Lady

# October 14

It is not the still calm of life,
or in the repose of a specific situation,
that great characters are formed.

Abigail Adams
1744-1818, American First Lady

# March 20

With each new experience of letting God be in control, we gain courage and reinforcement for daring to do it again and again.

GLORIA GAITHER
1942–, AMERICAN WRITER, SINGER/SONGWRITER

# October 13

You're not obligated to win. You're obligated to keep trying to do the best you can every day.

MARION WRIGHT EDELMAN
1939–, AMERICAN ATTORNEY, CIVIL RIGHTS ACTIVIST

# March 21

Make the least of all that goes and
the most of all that comes. Don't regret what
is past. Cherish what you have. Look forward to
all that is to come. And most important
of all, rely moment by moment on Jesus.

GIGI GRAHAM TCHIVIDJIAN
1945–, AMERICAN WRITER, SPEAKER, D. BILLY GRAHAM

# October 12

**Here's the test of the reality of your faith: on whom does your life depend?**

Elisabeth Elliot
1926–, American writer,
m. martyred missionary Jim Elliot

*Steep yourself in God-reality, God-initiative, God-provisions. You'll find all your everyday human concerns will be met. Don't be afraid of missing out. You're my dearest friends! The Father wants to give you the very kingdom itself.*

Luke 12:28 The Message

# March 22

**Nothing great was ever done without much enduring.**

Catherine of Siena
1347-1380, Italian Christian

*My brothers and sisters, whenever you face trials of any kind, consider it nothing but joy...and let endurance have its full effect, so that you may be mature and complete, lacking in nothing.*

JAMES 1:2,4 NRSV

# October 11

God has put into each of our lives a void that cannot be filled by the world. We may leave God or put Him on hold, but He is always there, patiently waiting for us...to turn back to Him.

EMILIE BARNES
1938-, AMERICAN SPEAKER, WRITER

# March 23

We must not, in trying to think about how we can make a big difference, ignore the small daily differences we can make which, over time, add up to big differences that we often cannot foresee.

Marion Wright Edelman
1939-, American attorney, civil rights activist

# October 10

**No one can make you feel inferior without your consent.**

Eleanor Roosevelt
1884–1962, American First Lady, humanitarian

# March 24

With God, life is eternal—both in quality and length. There is no joy comparable to the joy of discovering something new from God, about God. If the continuing life is a life of joy, we will go on discovering, learning.

Eugenia Price
1916-1996, American writer

# October 9

Often I have made a request of God
with earnest pleadings even backed up with
Scripture, only to have Him say "No"
because He had something better in store.

Ruth Bell Graham
1920–2007, American writer, m. Billy Graham

# March 25

It is God to whom and with whom we travel,
and while He is the End of our journey,
He is also at every stopping place.

ELISABETH ELLIOT
1926–, AMERICAN WRITER,
M. MARTYRED MISSIONARY JIM ELLIOT

# October 8

**If the world seems cold to you, kindle fires to warm it.**

LUCY LARCOM
1824–1893, AMERICAN EDITOR, POET, MILL WORKER

# March 26

The Lord's chief desire is to reveal Himself to you and, in order for Him to do that, He gives you abundant grace. The Lord gives you the experience of enjoying His presence. He touches you, and His touch is so delightful that, more than ever, you are drawn inwardly to Him.

Madame Jeanne Guyon
1648-1717, French Christian

# October 7

Dear friends, I just dream one day people all over the world can live in real peace—no fighting, and no hostility. We should work together to build peace and happiness for all people in all nations.

KIM PHUC
1963–, VIETNAM WAR SURVIVOR OF NAPALM BOMB

*Be of one mind, live in peace; and the God of love and peace shall be with you.*

II CORINTHIANS 13:11 KJV

# March 27

Obstacles are those frightful things you see when you take your eyes off the goal.

HANNAH MORE
1745–1833, BRITISH WRITER, SOCIAL REFORMER

*Don't worry about anything; instead, pray about everything; tell God your needs and...thank Him for His answers.*

PHILIPPIANS 4:6–7 TLB

# October 6

When I look back at where I've been,
I see that what I am becoming is a whole lot
further down the road from where I was.

Gloria Gaither
1942–, American writer, singer/songwriter

# March 28

Love is the divine vitality that everywhere produces and restores life. To each and every one of us, it gives the power of working miracles if we will.

LYDIA MARIE CHILD
1802-1880, AMERICAN ABOLITIONIST, WRITER

# October 5

It is not my business to think about myself.
My business is to think about God.
It is for God to think about me.

Simone Weil
1909-1943, French revolutionary, philosopher

# March 29

It is not how many years we live,
but what we do with them.

Catherine Booth
1829-1890, British evangelist,
first woman Salvation Army general

# October 4

So often we think that to be encouragers we have to produce great words of wisdom when, in fact, a few simple syllables of sympathy and an arm around the shoulder can often provide much needed comfort.

Florence Littauer
1928-, American speaker, writer

# March 30

God's way of dealing with us [is] to throw us into situations over our depth, then supply us with the necessary ability to swim.

CATHERINE MARSHALL
1914–1983, AMERICAN WRITER

# October 3

As God's standard of everything is high, let us endeavor to live for Him with the highest intention in mind.

HANNAH MORE
1745-1833, BRITISH WRITER, SOCIAL REFORMER

# March 31

Intricately woven, a blanket of stars covers the night sky, each star set in its place, reflecting its perfect light. All the stars together make a grand display, glimmering and shimmering in a unique expression of praise to the Creator of them all.

WENDY MOORE
1971–, AMERICAN WRITER

# October 2

**Men judge us by the success of our efforts. God looks at the efforts themselves.**

Charlotte Brontë
1816–1855, British writer

*Do you want to stand out? Then step down. Be a servant. If you puff yourself up, you'll get the wind knocked out of you. But if you're content to simply be yourself, your life will count for plenty.*

MATTHEW 23:11–12 The Message

# April 1

Never be afraid to trust an unknown future to an all-knowing God.

Corrie ten Boom
1892–1983, Dutch evangelist, writer

# October 1

It's simple things, like a glowing sunset, the sound of a running stream or the fresh smell in a meadow that cause us to pause and marvel at the wonder of life, to contemplate its meaning and significance. Who can hold an autumn leaf in their hand, or sift the warm white sand on the beach, and not wonder at the Creator of it all?

WENDY MOORE
1971–, AMERICAN WRITER

# April 2

No trumpets sound when the important decisions of our life are made. Destiny is made known silently.

Agnes DeMille
1905–1993, American dancer, choreographer

# September 30

If I can think of myself as loved, I can love and accept others. If I see myself as forgiven, I can be gracious toward others. If I see myself as powerful, I can do what I know is right. If I see myself as full, I can give myself freely to others.

KATHY PEEL
1951–, AMERICAN WRITER

# April 3

To put yourself in another's place requires real imagination, but by so doing each Girl Scout will be able to live among others happily.

Juliette Low,
1860-1927, British/American humanitarian,
founder of Girl Scouts of America

# September 29

God gave me my gifts. I will do all I can to show Him how grateful I am to Him.

GRACE LIVINGSTON HILL
1865–1947, AMERICAN WRITER

# April 4

Everyone has inside herself a piece of good news! The good news is that you really don't know how great you can be, how much you can love, what you can accomplish and what your potential is.

Anne Frank
1929-1945, German Jewish diarist

*Isn't everything you have and everything you are sheer gifts from God?... You already have all you need.*

I CORINTHIANS 4:7-8 The Message

# September 28

Gratitude unlocks the fullness of life. It turns what we have into enough, and more. It turns denial into acceptance, chaos to order, confusion to clarity. It can turn a meal into a feast, a house into a home, a stranger into a friend. Gratitude makes sense of our past, brings peace for today, and creates a vision for tomorrow.

Melody Beattie
1948-, American writer, speaker

# April 5

Spend all you have for loveliness,
Buy it and never count the cost;
For one white singing hour of peace
Count many a year of strife well lost,
And for a breath of ecstasy
Give all you have been, or could be.

SARA TEASDALE
1884–1933, AMERICAN POET

# September 27

How we leave the world is more important than how we enter it.

Janette Oke
1935–, American writer

*May you be given more and more of God's kindness, peace, and love.*

JUDE 1:2 TLB

# April 6

Spring bursts today,
For love is risen
and all the earth's at play.

Christina Rossetti
1830-1894, British poet, lyricist

# September 26

One way or the other, God, who thought up the family in the first place, has the very best idea of how to bring sense to the chaos of broken relationships we see all around us. I really believe that if I remain still and listen a lot, He will share some solutions with me so I can share them with others.

Jill Briscoe
1935–, American speaker, writer

# April 7

We are of such value to God that He came to live among us...and to guide us home. He will go to any length to seek us, even to being lifted high upon the cross to draw us back to Himself. We can only respond by loving God for His love.

Catherine of Siena
1347-1380, Italian Christian

# September 25

Individuals can change things....
If everyone will just do their little part,
then we can make a tremendous difference
in the lives of other people.

SARAH PURCELL
1970–, AMERICAN WRITER

# April 8

One can get just as much exultation in losing oneself in a little thing as in a big thing. It is nice to think how one can be recklessly lost in a daisy!

ANNE MORROW LINDBERGH
1906-2001, AMERICAN WRITER, M. CHARLES LINDBERGH

# September 24

When you are truly joined in spirit,
another woman's good is your good too.
You work for the good of each other.

RUTH SENTER
1944–, AMERICAN WRITER

# April 9

Leadership should be born out of the understanding of the needs of those who would be affected by it.

MARIAN ANDERSON
1897-1993, AMERICAN SINGER

*A wise person gets known for insight; gracious words add to one's reputation.*

PROVERBS 16:21 THE MESSAGE

# September 23

What constitutes success? She has achieved success who has lived well; laughed often and loved much; who has gained the respect of intelligent people and the love of little children; who has filled her niche and accomplished her task; who has left the world better than she found it; who has always looked for the best in others and given the best she had.

BESSIE ANDERSON STANLEY
?-1952, AMERICAN WRITER

# April 10

The human heart, has hidden treasures,
In secret kept, in silence sealed;—
The thoughts, the hopes, the dreams, the pleasures,
Whose charms were broken if revealed.

CHARLOTTE BRONTË
1816-1855, BRITISH WRITER

# September 22

You don't just luck into things as much as you'd like to think you do. You build them step by step, whether it's friendships or opportunities.

Barbara Bush
1925–, American First Lady

# April 11

I am convinced beyond a shadow
of any doubt that the most valuable pursuit
we can embark upon is to know God.

Kay Arthur
1933-, American writer

# September 21

Not everyone possesses boundless energy or a conspicuous talent. We are not equally blessed with great intellect or physical beauty or emotional strength. But we have all been given the same ability to be faithful.

GIGI GRAHAM TCHIVIDJIAN
1945–, AMERICAN WRITER, SPEAKER, D. BILLY GRAHAM

# April 12

God wears Himself out through the infinite thickness of time and space in order to reach the soul and to captivate it.... The soul, starting from the opposite end, makes the same journey that God made towards it. And that is the cross.

Simone Weil
1909-1943, French revolutionary, philosopher

# September 20

There is no such thing as can't, only won't. If you're qualified, all it takes is a burning desire to accomplish, to make a change. Go forward, go backward. Whatever it takes! But you can't blame other people or society in general. It all comes from your mind. When we do the impossible we realize we are special people.

JAN ASHFORD
1932–, AMERICAN BUSINESSWOMAN

# April 13

Modern invention has banished the spinning-wheel, and the same law of progress makes the woman of today a different woman from her grandmother.

Susan B. Anthony
1820-1906, American suffragist

# September 19

God who is Goodness and Truth is also Beauty. It is this innate human and divine longing, found in the company of goodness and truth, that is able to recognize and leap up at beauty and rejoice and know that all is beautiful, that there is not one speck of beauty under the sun that does not mirror back the beauty of God.

Roberta Bondi
Contemporary, American educator, writer

# April 14

Helping one another is part
of the religion of our sisterhood.

LOUISA MAY ALCOTT
1832–1888, AMERICAN WRITER

*May God who gives patience, steadiness, and encouragement help you to live in complete harmony with each other.*

ROMANS 15:5 TLB

# September 18

Women don't want a divided life.... They recognize that career is not enough; they want to be interconnected with people. They want to keep growing throughout their lives, adjusting as needed to different circumstances. They want to live a balanced life.

Mary Ellen Ashcroft
1952–, American fiction writer

# April 15

It is easier to gaze into the sun,
than into the face of the mystery of God.
Such is its beauty and its radiance.

HILDEGARD OF BINGEN
1098-1179, GERMAN NUN, CHRISTIAN POET

# September 17

The most important aspect is to be yourself
and have confidence in yourself....
Triumph can't be had without the struggle.

Wilma Rudolph
1940–1994, American Olympic gold medalist

*Our God gives you everything you need, makes you everything you're to be.*

II THESSALONIANS 1:2 The Message

# April 16

There is nothing like staying
at home for real comfort.

Jane Austen
1775-1817, British writer

# September 16

A soul cannot live without loving.
It must have something to love,
for it was created to love.

Catherine of Siena
1347–1380, Italian Christian

# April 17

Hold fast your dreams!
Within your heart
Keep one still, secret spot
Where dreams may go
And, sheltered so,
May thrive and grow
Where doubt and fear are not.
O keep a place apart,
Within your heart,
For little dreams to go!

LOUISE DRISCOLL
1875-1957, AMERICAN POET, WRITER

# September 15

Everyone has a gift for something,
even if it is the gift of being a good friend.

MARIAN ANDERSON
1897–1993, AMERICAN SINGER

*God has given each of you some special abilities; be sure to use them to help each other, passing on to others God's many kinds of blessings.*

I PETER 4:10 TLB

# April 18

There may be no trumpet sound or loud applause when we make a right decision, just a calm sense of resolution and peace.

Gloria Gaither
1942-, American writer, singer/songwriter

# September 14

There can be no happiness if
the things we believe in are
different from the things we do.

Freya Madeline Stark
1893-1993, British writer, traveler

# April 19

**Truth does not change according to our ability to stomach it emotionally.**

Flannery O'Connor
1925-1964, American writer

*Don't become so well-adjusted to your culture that you fit into it without even thinking. Instead, fix your attention on God. You'll be changed from the inside out.... Unlike the culture around you, always dragging you down to its level of immaturity, God brings the best out of you, develops well-formed maturity in you.*

ROMANS 12:2 The Message

# September 13

I like living. I have sometimes been wildly, despairingly, acutely miserable, racked with sorrow, but through it all I still know quite certainly that just to be alive is a grand thing.

Agatha Christie
1890-1976, British mystery writer, playwright

# April 20

When indeed shall we learn that we are all related one to the other, that we are all members of one body? Until the spirit of love for our fellow man, regardless of race, color or creed, shall fill the world, making real in our lives and our deeds the actuality of human brotherhood—until the great mass of the people shall be filled with the sense of responsibility for each other's welfare, social justice can never be attained.

Helen Keller
1880-1968, American writer,
crusader for the handicapped

# September 12

An effort made for the happiness of others lifts us above ourselves.

LYDIA MARIE CHILD
1802–1880, AMERICAN ABOLITIONIST, WRITER

# April 21

The God of the universe—the One who created everything and holds it all in His hand—created each of us in His image, to bear His likeness, His imprint. It is only when Christ dwells within our hearts, radiating the pure light of His love through our humanity, that we discover who we are and what we were intended to be. There is no other joy that reaches as deep or as wide or as high—there is no other joy that is more complete.

Wendy Moore
1971-, American writer

# September 11

The best reason to pray is that God
is really there. In praying, our unbelief
gradually starts to melt. God moves smack
into the middle of even an ordinary day....
Prayer is a matter of keeping at it....
Thunderclaps and lightning flashes are very
unlikely. It is well to start small and quietly.

EMILIE GRIFFIN
CONTEMPORARY, AMERICAN WRITER

# April 22

I don't think there is anyone who needs God's help and grace as much as I do. Sometimes I feel so helpless and weak. I think that is why God uses me. Because I cannot depend on my own strength, I rely on Him twenty-four hours a day.

Mother Teresa of Calcutta
1910–1997, Roman Catholic nun,
Nobel Peace Prize winner

# September 10

The beauty of a woman
is not in a facial mole,
But true beauty in a woman
is reflected in her soul.
It is the caring that she lovingly gives,
the passion that she shows,
And the beauty of a woman
with passing years—only grows!

AUDREY HEPBURN
1929-1993, BELGIAN ACTOR

*A kindhearted woman gains respect.*

PROVERBS 11:16 NIV

# April 23

I do not know anyone who has got to the top
without hard work. That is the recipe.
It will not always get you to the top,
but it should get you pretty near.

Margaret Thatcher
1925-, former Prime Minister of Great Britain

# September 9

People see God every day, they just don't recognize Him.

Pearl Bailey
1918-1990, American singer

# April 24

The woman who creates and sustains a home,
and under whose hands children grow up
to be strong and pure men and women,
is a creator second only to God.

Helen Hunt Jackson
1830-1855, American writer, Indian rights reformer

*And God is able to make all grace abound to you,
so that in all things at all times, having all that you need,
you will abound in every good work.*

II CORINTHIANS 9:8 NIV

# September 8

My precious family and friends have taught me
that joy and sorrow, storms and sunshine,
tears and laughter are all part of living—
and the sun does shine on the other side.

MARGARET JENSEN
1916-2007, CANADIAN WRITER

# April 25

Far rather would I sit and sew
beside my poor mother, for this thing
is not of my condition. But I must go,
and I must do this thing, because my Lord
will have it so. Rather now than tomorrow,
and tomorrow than the day after!

Joan of Arc
1412–1431, French patriot and martyr

# September 7

**You pay God a compliment by asking great things of Him.**

Teresa of Avila
1515-1582, Spanish Christian writer

# April 26

By putting the gift of yearning for God into every human being's heart, God at the same time draws all people made in God's image to God's self and into their own true selves.

Roberta Bondi
Contemporary, American educator, writer

# September 6

In all ranks of life the human heart yearns for the beautiful; and the beautiful things that God makes are His gift to all alike.

Harriet Beecher Stowe
1811–1896, American writer

# April 27

The very act of planting a seed in the earth has in it to me something beautiful. I always do it with a joy that is largely mixed with awe.

Celia Laighton Thaxter
1835-1894, American poet

# September 5

**Earth is crammed with heaven.**

ELIZABETH BARRETT BROWNING
1806–1861, BRITISH POET

*The Lord will guide you always; He will satisfy your needs.... You will be like a well-watered garden, like a spring whose waters never fail.*

ISAIAH 58:11 NIV

# April 28

Love the moment. Flowers grow
out of dark moments. Therefore,
each moment is vital. It affects the whole.
Life is a succession of such moments
and to live each is to succeed.

Corita Kent
1918-1986, American artist

# September 4

Freedom is not the right to do what we want
but the power to do what we ought.

Corrie ten Boom
1892–1983, Dutch evangelist, writer

# April 29

A good laugh is as good as a prayer sometimes.

Lucy Maud Montgomery
1874–1942, Canadian writer

*She is clothed with strength and dignity; she can laugh at the days to come.*

PROVERBS 31:25 NIV

# September 3

Faith and doubt both are needed—
not as antagonists, but working side by side—
to take us around the unknown curve.

Lillian Smith
1897-1966, American educator, writer, social activist

# April 30

Youth is, after all, just a moment, but it is the moment, the spark that you always carry in your heart.

RAISA GORBACHEV
1932-1999, RUSSIAN, USSR FIRST LADY

# September 2

We are so preciously loved by God that we cannot even comprehend it. No created being can ever know how much and how sweetly and tenderly God loves them.

Julian of Norwich
1342-1413, British Christian

# May 1

The God who created, names,
and numbers the stars in the heavens
also numbers the hairs of my head....
He pays attention to very big things
and to very small ones. What matters to me
matters to Him, and that changes my life.

Elisabeth Elliot
1926–, American writer,
m. martyred missionary Jim Elliot

# September 1

I never see what has been done;
I only see what remains to be done.

Marie Curie
1867-1934, Polish-born French physicist

# May 2

If you are unhappy with your lot in life,
build a service station on it.

Corrie ten Boom
1892–1983, Dutch evangelist, writer

# August 31

When we do what is right, we have contentment, peace, and happiness.

BEVERLY LAHAYE
1929–, AMERICAN WRITER

*Knowing what is right is like a deep water in the heart; a wise person draws from the well within.*

PROVERBS 20:5 THE MESSAGE

# May 3

I am a big believer that you have to nourish any relationship. I am still very much a part of my friends' lives and they are very much a part of my life.

NANCY REAGAN
1921–, AMERICAN FIRST LADY, ACTOR

# August 30

Go outside, to the fields, enjoy nature and the sunshine, go out and try to recapture happiness in yourself and in God. Think of all the beauty that's still left in and around you and be happy!

Anne Frank
1929–1945, German Jewish diarist

# May 4

The most practical thing in the world is common sense and common humanity.

LADY NANCY ASTOR
1879-1964, BRITISH,
FIRST WOMAN MEMBER OF PARLIAMENT

*Dear friend, guard Clear Thinking and Common Sense with your life; don't for a minute lose sight of them. They'll keep your soul alive and well, they'll keep you fit and attractive.*

PROVERBS 3:21-22 THE MESSAGE

# August 29

To be a joy-bearer and a joy-giver says everything, for in our life, if one is joyful, it means that one is faithfully living for God, and that nothing else counts; and if one gives joy to others one is doing God's work; with joy without and joy within, all is well.... I can conceive no higher way.

JANET ERSKINE STUART
1857-1914, BRITISH MEMBER OF
RELIGIOUS OF THE SACRED HEART

# May 5

Those who contemplate the beauty of the earth find reserves of strength that will endure as long as life lasts. There is symbolic as well as actual beauty in the migration of the birds, the ebb and flow of the tides, the folded bud ready for the spring. There is something infinitely healing in the repeated refrains of nature—the assurance that dawn comes after night, and spring after the winter.

RACHEL CARSON
1907-1964, AMERICAN BIOLOGIST, WRITER

# August 28

We don't need soft skies to make friendship a joy to us. What a heavenly thing it is; World without end, truly. I grow warm thinking of it, and should glow at the thought if all the glaciers of the Alps were heaped over me! Such friends God has given me in this little life of mine!

Celia Laighton Thaxter
1835-1894, American poet

# May 6

We are so busy in our lives that we need to purposely give attention to the everyday things that can make our lives lovelier, such as keeping a vase of fresh flowers in an obvious place, or several places in the house. Planting roses or other flowers for this purpose makes sense.

EMILIE BARNES
1938-, AMERICAN SPEAKER, WRITER

# August 27

The purpose of life, after all, is to live it, to taste experience to the utmost, to reach out eagerly without fear for newer and richer experiences.

Eleanor Roosevelt
1884–1962, American First Lady, humanitarian

# May 7

Let every woman become so cultivated and refined in intellect, that her taste and judgment will be respected...so unassuming and unambitious, that collision and competition will be banished... then, the fathers, the husbands, and the sons, will find an influence thrown around them, to which they will yield not only willingly but proudly.

CATHERINE BEECHER
1800-1878, AMERICAN EDUCATOR

# August 26

The music soars within the little lark,
And the lark soars.

ELIZABETH BARRETT BROWNING
1806–1861, BRITISH POET

*You have done so much for me, O Lord.*
*No wonder I am glad! I sing for joy. O Lord,*
*what miracles You do! And how deep are Your thoughts!*

PSALM 92:4–5 TLB

# May 8

The splendor of the rose and the whiteness of the lily do not rob the little violet of its scent nor the daisy of its simple charm. If every tiny flower wanted to be a rose, spring would lose its loveliness.

Therese of Lisieux
1873-1897, French Carmelite nun

# August 25

I share Einstein's affirmation that anyone who is not lost on the rapturous awe at the power and glory of the mind behind the universe "is as good as a burnt out candle."

MADELEINE L'ENGLE
1918-2007, AMERICAN WRITER

# May 9

May your life become one of glad and unending praise to the Lord as you journey through this world, and in the world that is to come!

Teresa of Avila
1515–1582, Spanish Christian writer

*You've always been great toward me—what love!... You, O God, are both tender and kind, not easily angered, immense in love, and You never, never quit.*

PSALM 86:13,15 The Message

# August 24

All creatures have something visible and invisible. The visible is weak; the invisible is strong and alive. This [the invisible] seeks to get through to human understanding because human beings do not see it. And yet these invisible realities are forces in the workings of the Holy Spirit.

HILDEGARD OF BINGEN
1098-1179, GERMAN NUN, CHRISTIAN POET

# May 10

For whatever life holds for you and your family in the coming days, weave the unfailing fabric of God's Word through your heart and mind. It will hold strong, even if the rest of life unravels.

Gigi Graham Tchividjian
1945–, American writer, speaker, d. Billy Graham

# August 23

Expressed affection is the best of all methods to use when you want to light a glow in someone's heart and to feel it in your own.

RUTH STAFFORD PEALE
1906–2008, AMERICAN WRITER,
CO-FOUNDER FOUNDATION FOR CHRISTIAN LIVING

# May 11

We plant seeds that will flower
as results in our lives, so best to
remove the weeds of anger, avarice,
envy and doubt, that peace and
abundance may manifest for all.

DOROTHY DAY
1897-1980, AMERICAN WRITER, SOCIAL REFORMER

# August 22

I long to put the experience of fifty years at once into your young lives, to give you at once the key to that treasure chamber every gem of which has cost me tears and struggles and prayers, but you must work for these inward treasures yourselves.

HARRIET BEECHER STOWE
1811-1896, AMERICAN WRITER

# May 12

If I'm not free to fail, I'm not free to take risks, and everything in life that's worth doing involves a willingness to take a risk and involves the risk of failure....I have to try, but I do not have to succeed.

Madeleine L'Engle
1918-2007, American writer

# August 21

We never know how high we are
Till we are called to rise;
And then, if we are true to plan,
Our statures touch the skies.

EMILY DICKINSON
1830–1886, AMERICAN POET

*Finally...whatever is true, whatever is honorable, whatever is right, whatever is pure, whatever is lovely, whatever is of good repute, if there is any excellence and if anything worthy of praise, let your mind dwell on these things.*

PHILIPPIANS 4:8–9 NIV

# May 13

In a world where there is so much
to be done, I felt strongly impressed
that there must be something for me to do.

Dorothea Dix
1802-1887, American humanitarian and reformer

# August 20

Find the passion. It takes great passion and great energy to do anything creative. I would go so far as to say you can't do it without that passion.

Agnes DeMille
1905-1993, American dancer, choreographer

# May 14

The beauty of a woman
is not in the clothes she wears,
The figure that she carries,
or the way she combs her hair.
The beauty of a woman
must be seen from in her eyes,
Because that is the doorway to her heart,
the place where love resides.

AUDREY HEPBURN
1929-1993, BELGIAN ACTOR

*Cultivate inner beauty, the gentle, gracious kind that God delights in.*

I PETER 3:4 THE MESSAGE

# August 19

To follow without halt, one aim; there is the
secret of success. And success? What is it?
I do not find it in the applause of the theater.
It lies rather in the satisfaction of accomplishment.

Anna Pavlova
1881-1931, Russian ballerina

# May 15

You find yourself refreshed by
the presence of cheerful people.
Why not make an honest effort
to confer that pleasure on others?
Half the battle is gained if you never
allow yourself to say anything gloomy.

Lydia Marie Child
1802-1880, American abolitionist, writer

# August 18

It is my calling to treat every human being with grace and dignity, to treat every person, whether encountered in a palace or a gas station, as a life made in the image of God.

Sheila Walsh
1956-, American singer, speaker

# May 16

Giving encouragement to others is a most welcome gift, for the results of it are lifted spirits, increased self-worth, and a hopeful future.

FLORENCE LITTAUER
1928–, AMERICAN SPEAKER, WRITER

# August 17

Money doesn't give you any license to relax.
It gives an opportunity to use all your abilities,
free of financial worries, to go forward, and to use
your superior advantages and talents to help others.

Rose Fitzgerald Kennedy
1890-1995, mother of John F. Kennedy

# May 17

Because I have a heart for God I also have a heart for women. As I hear their stories, I realize so many feel themselves to be inadequate. What a joy it is to believe them into doing those things they never believed they could do and being the people they never believed they could be.

Jill Briscoe
1935–, American speaker, writer

# August 16

Our Lord does not care so much
for the importance of our works
as for the love with which they are done.

TERESA OF AVILA
1515-1582, SPANISH CHRISTIAN WRITER

*The ways of right-living people glow with light;*
*the longer they live, the brighter they shine....*
*Keep vigilant watch over your heart; that's where life starts.*

PROVERBS 4:18,23 THE MESSAGE

# May 18

Love is extravagant in the price it
is willing to pay, the time it is willing to give,
the hardships it is willing to endure, and the
strength it is willing to spend. Love never thinks
in terms of "how little," but always in terms of
"how much." Love gives, love knows, and love lasts.

Joni Eareckson Tada
1949–, American writer, speaker

# August 15

I would like to be known as a person who is concerned about freedom and equality and justice and prosperity for all people.

Rosa Parks
1913-2005, American civil rights activist

# May 19

That it will never come again is what makes life so sweet.

EMILY DICKINSON
1830-1886, AMERICAN POET

*Pursue a righteous life—a life of wonder, faith, love, steadiness, courtesy. Run hard and fast in the faith. Seize the eternal life, the life you were called to.*

I TIMOTHY 6:11-12 THE MESSAGE

# August 14

Blessed are those who can give without remembering and take without forgetting.

Elizabeth Bibesco
1897-1945, British writer, poet

# May 20

Love works in ways that are wondrous and strange,
There is nothing in life that Love cannot change.

HELEN STEINER RICE
1900-1981, AMERICAN POET

# August 13

God…is greater than your problems. He can solve them all. Put your trust in Him and you will experience this.

Basilea Schlink
1904-2001, German nun, writer

# May 21

God delights to meet the faith of one who looks up to Him and says, "Lord, You know that I cannot do this—but I believe that You can!"

Amy Carmichael
1867–1951, Irish missionary to India, poet

# August 12

You must accept that you might fail; then, if you do your best and still don't win, at least you can be satisfied that you've tried. If you don't accept failure as a possibility, you don't set high goals, you don't branch out, you don't try—you don't take the risk.

ROSALYNN CARTER
1927–, AMERICAN FIRST LADY

# May 22

At the end of your life you will never regret not having passed one more test, not winning one more verdict, or not closing one more deal. You will regret time not spent with a husband, a friend, a child, or a parent.

Barbara Bush
1925–, American First Lady

# August 11

It is always possible to be thankful for what is given rather than to complain about what is not given. One or the other becomes a habit of life.

ELISABETH ELLIOT
1926–, AMERICAN WRITER,
M. MARTYRED MISSIONARY JIM ELLIOT

*In every thing give thanks.*

I THESSALONIANS 5:18 KJV

# May 23

Success can make you go one of two ways. It can make you a prima donna—or it can smooth the edges, take away the insecurities, let the nice things come out.

BARBARA WALTERS
1929–, AMERICAN BROADCAST JOURNALIST

# August 10

Achievement is the knowledge that you have studied and worked hard and done the best that is in you. Success is being praised by others, and that's nice, too, but not as important or satisfying. Always aim for achievement and forget about success.

Helen Hayes
1900-1993, American actor

# May 24

God is everything that is good and comfortable for us. He is our clothing that for love wraps us, clasps us, and all surrounds us for tender love.

JULIAN OF NORWICH
1342-1413, BRITISH CHRISTIAN

*For God is sheer beauty, all-generous in love, loyal always and ever.*

PSALM 100:5 THE MESSAGE

# August 9

We would have every arbitrary barrier thrown down. We would have every path laid open to women as freely as to men.

Margaret Fuller
1810-1850, American writer

# May 25

Women observe subconsciously a thousand little details, without knowing they are doing so. Their subconscious mind adds these little things together—and they call the result intuition.

Agatha Christie
1890-1976, British mystery writer, playwright

# August 8

God loves me as God loves all people, without qualification.... To be in the image of God means that all of us are made for the purpose of knowing and loving God and one another and of being loved in turn, not literally in the same way God knows and loves, but in a way appropriate to human beings.

Roberta Bondi
Contemporary, American educator, writer

# May 26

The things that matter the most in this world,
they can never be held in our hand.

Gloria Gaither
1942-, American writer, singer/songwriter

# August 7

Choices can change our lives profoundly. The choice to mend a broken relationship, to say "yes" to a difficult assignment, to lay aside some important work to play with a child, to visit some forgotten person—these small choices may affect many lives eternally.

Gloria Gaither
1942-, American writer, singer/songwriter

# May 27

God looks at the world through
the eyes of love. If we, therefore,
as human beings made in the image
of God also want to see reality rationally,
that is, as it truly is, then we, too,
must learn to look at what we see with love.

Roberta Bondi
Contemporary, American educator, writer

# August 6

Happiness comes of the capacity
to feel deeply, to enjoy simply,
to think freely, to risk life, to be needed.

Storm (Margaret) Jameson
1891–1986, British writer

*The Lord your God...will take great delight in you,*
*He will quiet you with His love, He will rejoice over you with singing.*

ZEPHANIAH 3:17 NIV

# May 28

If we would build on a sure foundation
in friendship we must love friends
for their sake rather than our own.

Charlotte Brontë
1816-1855, British writer

# August 5

Love is something like the clouds that were in the sky before the sun came out. You cannot touch the clouds, you know; but you feel the rain and know how glad the flowers and the thirsty earth are to have it after a hot day. You cannot touch love either; but you feel the sweetness that it pours into everything.

Annie Sullivan
1866-1936, American educator,
noted as Helen Keller's teacher

# May 29

Showing kindness to others is one of the nicest things we can do for ourselves.

Janette Oke
1935–, American writer

*He who refreshes others will himself be refreshed.*

PROVERBS 11:25 NIV

# August 4

It's easy to be independent when you've got money. But to be independent when you haven't got a thing—that's the Lord's test.

MAHALIA JACKSON
1911-1972, AMERICAN GOSPEL SINGER

# May 30

In spite of the cost of living, it's still popular.

KATHLEEN NORRIS
1947-, AMERICAN WRITER

# August 3

People say, "What is the sense of our small effort?" They cannot see that we must lay one brick at a time, take one step at a time.

Dorothy Day
1897–1980, American writer, social reformer

# May 31

After the verb “To Love”...
“To Help” is the most beautiful verb in the world.

Bertha von Suttner
1843-1914, writer, Nobel Peace Prize winner

# August 2

Life is not intended to be simply a round of work, no matter how interesting and important that work may be. A moment's pause to watch the glory of a sunrise or a sunset is soul satisfying, while a bird's song will set the steps to music all day long.

LAURA INGALLS WILDER
1867-1957, AMERICAN CHILDREN'S WRITER

# June 1

Oh better than the minting
Of a gold-crowned king
Is the safe-kept memory
Of a lovely thing.

SARA TEASDALE
1884-1933, AMERICAN POET

*May the Lord continually bless you with heaven's blessings as well as with human joys.*

PSALM 128:5 TLB

# August 1

Many persons have a wrong idea
of what constitutes real happiness.
It is not obtained through self-gratification,
but through fidelity to a worthy purpose.

HELEN KELLER
1880-1968, AMERICAN WRITER,
CRUSADER FOR THE HANDICAPPED

*To enjoy your work and to accept your lot in life–*
*that is indeed a gift from God.*

ECCLESIASTES 5:20 TLB

# June 2

We can never untangle all the woes
in other people's lives. We can't produce
miracles overnight. But we can bring
a cup of cool water to a thirsty soul,
or a scoop of laughter to a lonely heart.

BARBARA JOHNSON
1927-2007 AMERICAN WRITER, SPEAKER

# July 31

His tenderness in the springing grass,
His beauty in the flowers,
His living love in the sun above—
All here, and near, and ours.

Charlotte Perkins Gilman
1860-1935, American writer, social critic

# June 3

O the pure delight of a single hour
That before Thy throne I spend,
When I kneel in prayer,
and with Thee, my God,
I commune as friend with friend!

FANNY CROSBY
1820-1915, HYMN WRITER

# July 30

Just pray for a tough hide and a tender heart.

Ruth Bell Graham
1920-2007, American writer, m. Billy Graham

# June 4

A little praise is not only merest justice but is beyond the purse of no one.

Emily Post
1873-1960, American writer, socialite

# July 29

Don't let controversy hurt your soul.
Live near to God by prayer. Just fall down at
His feet and open your very soul before Him,
and throw yourself right into His arms.

Catherine Booth
1829-1890, British evangelist,
first woman Salvation Army general

# June 5

In today's world...it is still women's business to make life better, to make tomorrow better than today.

HELEN THAMES RALEY
1909-2002, AMERICAN WRITER

# July 28

From the world we see, hear, and touch, we behold inspired visions that reveal God's glory. In the sun's light, we catch warm rays of grace and glimpse His eternal design. In the birds' song, we hear His voice and it reawakens our need of Him. At the wind's touch, we feel His Spirit and sense our eternal existence.

WENDY MOORE
1971–, AMERICAN WRITER

# June 6

**Invest in the human soul. Who knows, it might be a diamond in the rough.**

MARY MCLEOD BETHUNE
1875–1955, AMERICAN EDUCATOR, WRITER

*Give generously, for your gifts will return to you later.*

ECCLESIASTES 11:1 TLB

# July 27

Prayer is not eloquence, but earnestness;
not the definition of helplessness,
but the feeling of it; not figures of
speech, but earnestness of soul.

HANNAH MORE
1745-1833, BRITISH WRITER, SOCIAL REFORMER

*Don't be weary in prayer; keep at it; watch for God's answers, and remember to be thankful when they come.*

COLOSSIANS 4:2 TLB

# June 7

The great thing about getting older is that you don't lose all the other ages you've been.

MADELEINE L'ENGLE
1918–2007, AMERICAN WRITER

# July 26

Allow your dreams a place in your prayers and plans. God-given dreams can help you move into the future He is preparing for you.

Barbara Johnson
1927-2007 American Writer, Speaker

# June 8

If you don't like the way the world is,
you change it. You have an obligation
to change it. You just do it one step at a time.

MARION WRIGHT EDELMAN
1939-, AMERICAN ATTORNEY, CIVIL RIGHTS ACTIVIST

# July 25

Open wide the windows of our spirits
and fill us full of light; open wide the door of
our hearts, that we may receive and entertain
Thee with all our powers of adoration.

Christina Rossetti
1830-1894, British poet, lyricist

# June 9

God has not promised skies always blue,
flower-strewn pathways all our lives through;
God has not promised sun without rain,
joy without sorrow, peace without pain.
But God has promised strength for the day,
rest for the labor, light for the way,
grace for the trials, help from above,
unfailing sympathy, undying love.

Annie Johnson Flint
1866-1932, American poet

# July 24

If we had no winter, the spring would not be so pleasant; if we did not sometimes taste of adversity, prosperity would not be so welcome.

ANNE BRADSTREET
1612-1672, AMERICAN WRITER

# June 10

Big doesn't necessarily mean better.
Sunflowers aren't better than violets.

EDNA FERBER
1885-1968, AMERICAN WRITER

# July 23

Civilization is a method of living,
an attitude of equal respect for all men.

Jane Addams
1860-1935, American social reformer,
Nobel Prize winner

# June 11

The basic experience of everyone
is the experience of human limitation.

FLANNERY O'CONNOR
1925-1964, AMERICAN WRITER

*Don't lose a minute in building on what you've been given,*
*complementing your basic faith with good character,*
*spiritual understanding, alert discipline, passionate patience,*
*reverent wonder, warm friendliness, and generous love,*
*each dimension fitting into and developing the others.*

II PETER 1:5 THE MESSAGE

# July 22

Nothing in life is to be feared. It is only to be understood.

Marie Curie
1867-1934, Polish-born French physicist

*O the depth of the riches and wisdom and knowledge of God!*

ROMANS 11:33 NRSV

# June 12

Take your work seriously, but never yourself.

Dame Margot Fonteyn
1919-1991, British ballerina

# July 21

To love what you do and feel that it matters—
how could anything be more fun?

KATHARINE GRAHAM
1917–2001, AMERICAN NEWSPAPER PUBLISHER

# June 13

Heavenly Father, Teach me not to procrastinate but to do what I can today, because there is no promise of tomorrow. Lead me to those people who are in need of something that I can give. I want to be available for You to use in any way that You should choose. Amen.

Kim Boyce
1963–, American singer, writer

# July 20

For God is, indeed, a wonderful Father who longs to pour out His mercy upon us, and whose majesty is so great that He can transform us from deep within.

Teresa of Avila
1515-1582, Spanish Christian writer

# June 14

In a special way, human beings...
being made in the image of God,
only become real human beings,
are only able to grow and thrive as
human beings as they also yearn for God.

Roberta Bondi
Contemporary, American educator, writer

# July 19

We rely upon the poets, the philosophers, and the playwrights to articulate what most of us can only feel, in joy or sorrow. They illuminate the thoughts for which we only grope.

HELEN HAYES
1900–1993, AMERICAN ACTOR

# June 15

The one thing that doesn't abide
by majority rule is a person's conscience.

Harper Lee
1926–, American writer, Pulitzer Prize winner

*Let love and faithfulness never leave you…*
*write them on the tablet of your heart.*

PROVERBS 3:3 NIV

# July 18

A happy woman is one who has no cares at all;
a cheerful woman is one who has cares
but doesn't let them get her down.

BEVERLY SILLS
1929-2007, AMERICAN OPERA SINGER

# June 16

Even if your efforts seem for years to be producing no result, one day a light that is in exact proportion to them will flood your soul.

SIMONE WEIL
1909–1943, FRENCH REVOLUTIONARY, PHILOSOPHER

# July 17

Love has its source in God,
for love is the very essence of His being.

KAY ARTHUR
1933-, AMERICAN WRITER

*God's love…is ever and always, eternally present.*

PSALM 103:17 THE MESSAGE

# June 17

Often God has to shut a door in our face,
so that He can subsequently open the door
through which He wants us to go.

CATHERINE MARSHALL
1914–1983, AMERICAN WRITER

# July 16

Failure is just another way to learn
how to do something right.

Marion Wright Edelman
1939-, American attorney, civil rights activist

# June 18

A ship in port is safe, but that is not what ships are for. Sail out to sea and do new things.

Grace Hopper
1906-1992, American computer programmer

# July 15

Every day we live is a priceless gift of God,
loaded with possibilities to learn
something new, to gain fresh insights.

Dale Evans Rogers
1912-2001, American actor, m. Roy Rogers

# June 19

A painting [is] a symbol for the universe. Inside it, each piece relates to the other. Each piece is only answerable to the rest of that little world. So, probably in the total universe, there is that kind of total harmony, but we get only little tastes of it.

Corita Kent
1918-1986, American artist

# July 14

If it can be verified, we don't need faith....
Faith is for that which lies on the
other side of reason. Faith is what makes
life bearable, with all its tragedies and
ambiguities and sudden, startling joys.

Madeleine L'Engle
1918-2007, American writer

# June 20

We do not need to search for heaven, over here or over there, in order to find our eternal Father. In fact, we do not even need to speak out loud, for though we speak in the smallest whisper or the most fleeting thought, He is close enough to hear us.

TERESA OF AVILA
1515-1582, SPANISH CHRISTIAN WRITER

*The Lord…is close to all who call on Him sincerely.*

PSALM 145:17-18 TLB

# July 13

[It wasn't] me, [it was] the Lord.
I always told Him, "I trust in You.
I don't know where to go or what to do,
but I expect You to lead me," and He always did.

HARRIET TUBMAN
1820–1913, AMERICAN ABOLITIONIST

# June 21

I believe the second half of one's life is meant to be better than the first half. The first half is finding out how you do it. And the second half is enjoying it.

Frances Lear
1923–1996, American businesswoman, publisher

# July 12

Courage...is when you know you're licked before you begin but you begin anyway and you see it through no matter what.

HARPER LEE
1926-, AMERICAN WRITER, PULITZER PRIZE WINNER

*Do not withhold good from those who deserve it, when it is in your power to act.*

PROVERBS 3:27 NIV

# June 22

If we just give God the little that we have,
we can trust Him to make it go around.

Gloria Gaither
1942–, American writer, singer/songwriter

# July 11

Goals are access lines to the future. They allow us to run the race with the finish line firmly established.

Emilie Barnes
1938–, American speaker, writer

# June 23

I am not afraid of storms for I am learning how to sail my ship.

Louisa May Alcott
1832-1888, American writer

# July 10

Only in growth, reform, and change, paradoxically enough, is true security to be found.

Anne Morrow Lindbergh
1906-2001, American writer; m. Charles Lindbergh

# June 24

What a circus we women perform every day of our lives. It puts a trapeze artist to shame.

Anne Morrow Lindbergh
1906–2001, American writer; m. Charles Lindbergh

# July 9

We all live with the objective of being happy; our lives are all different and yet the same.

Anne Frank
1929-1945, German Jewish diarist

# June 25

Because of their age-long training in human relations—for that is what feminine intuition really is—women have a special contribution to make to any group enterprise.

MARGARET MEAD
1901-1978, AMERICAN ANTHROPOLOGIST, WRITER

*She speaks with wisdom, and faithful instruction is on her tongue.*

PROVERBS 31:26 NIV

# July 8

Prayer is the way to open ourselves to God, and the way in which He shows us our unstable hearts and begins to strengthen them.

Teresa of Avila
1515–1582, Spanish Christian writer

*God's peace...is far more wonderful than the human mind can understand. His peace will keep your thoughts and your hearts quiet and at rest.*

PHILIPPIANS 4:7 TLB

# June 26

God is not in the vastness of greatness.
He is hid in the vastness of smallness.
He is not in the general. He is in the particular.

Pearl S. Buck
1892-1973, American writer, Nobel Prize winner

# July 7

We have a hunger of the mind which asks for knowledge of all around us; and the more we gain, the more is our desire. The more we see, the more we are capable of seeing.

Maria Mitchell
1818-1889, American astronomer, educator

# June 27

Wholehearted, ready laughter heals, encourages, relaxes anyone within hearing distance. The laughter that springs from love makes wide the space around it—gives room for the loved one to enter in. Real laughter welcomes, and never shuts out.

EUGENIA PRICE
1916–1996, AMERICAN WRITER

# July 6

You cannot make yourself feel
something you do not feel,
but you can make yourself do right
in spite of your feelings.

Pearl S. Buck
1892-1973, American writer, Nobel Prize winner

# June 28

For as the body is clad in the cloth, and the flesh in the skin, and the bones in the flesh, and the heart in the whole, so are we, soul and body, clad in the Goodness of God, and enclosed.

Julian of Norwich
1342-1413, British Christian

# July 5

I cannot count the number of times I have been strengthened by another woman's heartfelt hug, appreciative note, surprise gift, or caring questions.... My friends are an oasis to me, encouraging me to go on. They are essential to my well-being.

DEE BRESTIN
CONTEMPORARY, AMERICAN WRITER

# June 29

Happy people...enjoy the fundamental, often very simple things of life....They savor the moment, glad to be alive, enjoying their work, their families, the good things around them. They are adaptable; they can bend with the wind, adjust to the changes in their times, enjoy the contest of life....Their eyes are turned outward; they are aware, compassionate. They have the capacity to love.

JANE CANFIELD
CONTEMPORARY, AMERICAN WRITER

# July 4

Every formula which expresses a law of nature is a hymn of praise to God.

MARIA MITCHELL
1818–1889, AMERICAN ASTRONOMER, EDUCATOR

# June 30

What God gives in answer to our prayers
will always be the thing we most urgently need,
and it will always be sufficient.

Elisabeth Elliot
1926–, American writer,
m. martyred missionary Jim Elliot

# July 3

Isn't it splendid to think of all the things there are to find out about? It just makes me feel glad to be alive—it's such an interesting world. It wouldn't be half so interesting if we knew all about everything.

Lucy Maud Montgomery
1874-1942, Canadian writer

# July 2

Life is what we make it, always has been, always will be.

GRANDMA MOSES (ANNA MARY ROBERTSON)
1860–1961, AMERICAN ARTIST

*What happens when we live God's way? He brings gifts into our lives... things like affection for others, exuberance about life, serenity. We develop a willingness to stick with things, a sense of compassion in the heart, and a conviction that a basic holiness permeates things and people.*

GALATIANS 5:22–23 THE MESSAGE

# July 1

Like billowing clouds, like the incessant gurgle of the brook, the longing of the soul can never be stilled. It is this longing with which holy persons seek their work from God.

HILDEGARD OF BINGEN
1098-1179, GERMAN NUN, CHRISTIAN POET